D1216968

dabble lab

PAPER AIRPLANES
with a SIDE of SCIENCE

SPINNING BLIMP!

BEGINNING-LEVEL
Paper Airplanes
by Marie Buckingham

4D An Augmented Reading
Paper-Folding Experience

CAPSTONE PRESS
a capstone imprint

TABLE OF

CONTENTS

Download the Capstone 4D app!

Step 1 Ask an adult to search in the Apple App Store or Google Play for "Capstone 4D."

Step 2 Click Install (Android) or Get, then Install (Apple).

Step 3 Open the app.

Step 4 Scan any of the following spreads with this icon.

When you scan a spread, you'll find fun extra stuff to go with this book! You can also find these things on the web at *www.capstone4D.com* using the password: planes.blimp

FLIGHT TRAINING

Welcome to flight school! Here are a few basics you should know before diving in: Check the lightbulb boxes tucked alongside the project instructions for bite-size explanations of flight-science concepts related to your models. Check the photo boxes for tips on how to best launch your finished planes. Remember, there are four main forces that airplanes need to fly successfully: lift, weight, thrust, and drag. But the nine paper airplanes in this book need one more thing: YOU!

MATERIALS

Every paper airplane builder needs a well-stocked
toolbox. The models in this book use the materials
listed below. Take a minute before you begin folding
to gather what you need:

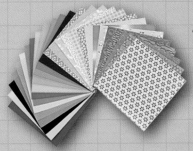

Paper

Any paper you can fold will work.
Notebook paper is always popular.
But paper with cool colors and designs
gives your planes style.

Scissors

Keep a scissors handy. Some models
need a snip here or there to fly well.

Paper Clips

Paper clips are perfect for adding
weight to a plane's nose. Keep a supply
of small and large paper clips on hand.

TECHNIQUES AND TERMS

Folding paper airplanes isn't difficult when you understand common folding techniques and terms. Review this list before folding the models in this book. Remember to refer back to this list if you get stuck on a tricky step.

Valley Folds

Valley folds are represented by a dashed line. The paper is creased along the line. The top surface of the paper is folded against itself like a book.

Mountain Folds

Mountain folds are represented by a pink or white dashed and dotted line. The paper is creased along the line and folded behind.

Reverse Folds

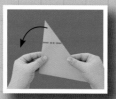  

Reverse folds are made by opening a pocket slightly and folding the model inside itself along existing creases.

Mark Folds

Mark folds are light folds used to make reference creases for a later step. Ideally, a mark fold will not be seen in the finished model.

Rabbit Ear Folds

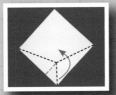

Rabbit ear folds are formed by bringing two edges of a point together using existing creases. The new point is folded to one side.

Squash Folds

Squash folds are formed by lifting one edge of a pocket and reforming it so the spine gets flattened. The existing creases become new edges.

FOLDING SYMBOLS

Fold the paper in the direction of the arrow.

Fold the paper behind.

Fold the paper and then unfold it.

Turn the paper over or rotate it to a new position.

A fold or edge hidden under another layer of paper; also used to mark where to cut with a scissors

DYNAMIC DART

Traditional Model

The Dynamic Dart is one of the most popular paper planes on the planet. It's the type of model that never lets you down. Best of all, its steps are super simple. You'll be folding it from memory in no time flat.

Materials

* 8.5- by 11-inch (22- by 28-centimeter) paper

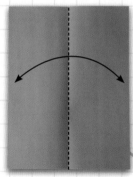

START HERE

1 Valley fold edge to edge and unfold.

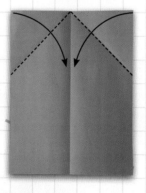

2 Valley fold the corners to the center.

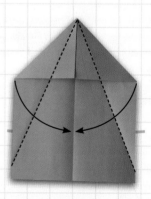

3 Valley fold the edges to the center.

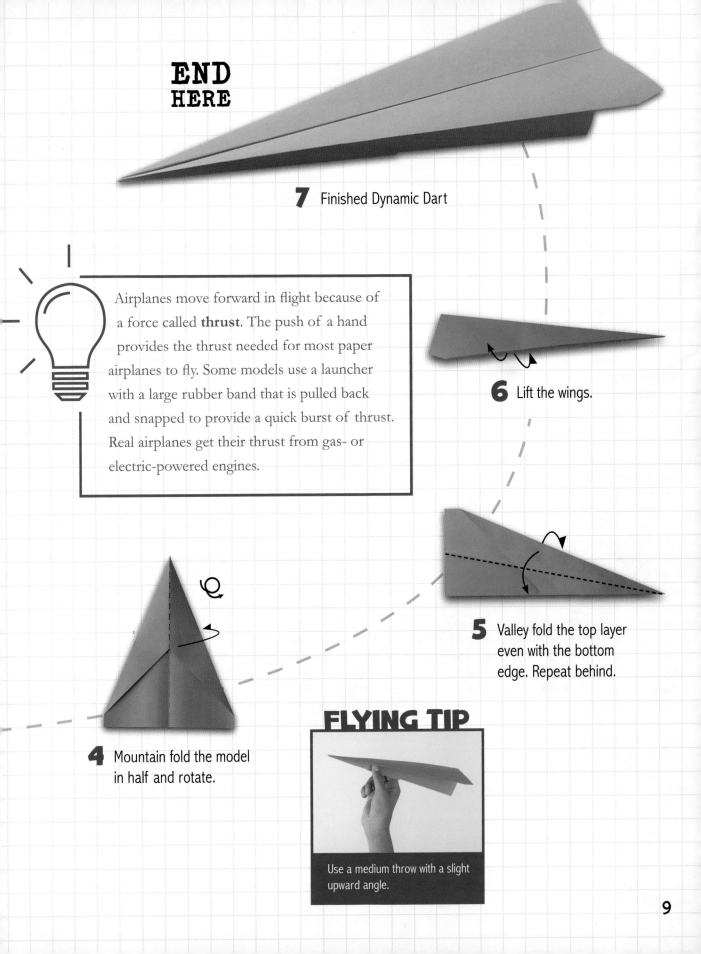

END
HERE

7 Finished Dynamic Dart

Airplanes move forward in flight because of a force called **thrust**. The push of a hand provides the thrust needed for most paper airplanes to fly. Some models use a launcher with a large rubber band that is pulled back and snapped to provide a quick burst of thrust. Real airplanes get their thrust from gas- or electric-powered engines.

6 Lift the wings.

5 Valley fold the top layer even with the bottom edge. Repeat behind.

4 Mountain fold the model in half and rotate.

FLYING TIP

Use a medium throw with a slight upward angle.

SPINNING BLIMP

Traditional Model

The Spinning Blimp is a clever paper toy. In your hand it looks like a ribbon. But in the air it spins so fast that it looks like a tiny blimp. Release it as high as you can and watch it twirl.

Materials

* 8.5- by 11-inch (22- by 28-cm) paper
* scissors

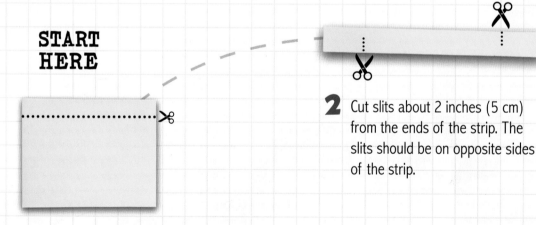

START HERE

1 Cut a 1.25-inch (3-cm) strip off the paper's long side.

2 Cut slits about 2 inches (5 cm) from the ends of the strip. The slits should be on opposite sides of the strip.

Pinch one side of the model's loop with your index finger and thumb. Release with a gentle forward push.

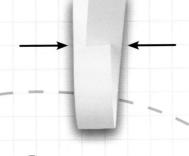

4 Slide the slits together to form a loop.

3 Bend the strip to bring the two slits together.

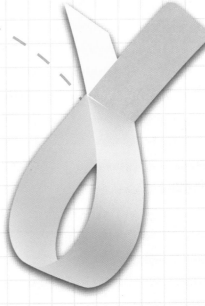

5 Finished Spinning Blimp

END HERE

Weight is a force that pulls a paper airplane (and everything else) down toward Earth. The force of weight is caused by Earth's gravity — or the pull of our planet. When thrust sends a paper airplane soaring through the air, the plane's weight will always bring it back down for a landing.

 # WHIRLY

Traditional Model

How can a simple paper strip be so much fun? With two small folds, the Whirly looks like a useless scrap of paper. But launch it once and you'll want to watch it flutter to the floor over and over again.

Materials

* 8.5- by 11-inch (22- by 28-cm) paper
* scissors

START HERE

1 Cut a 2.5-inch (6-cm) strip off the end of the paper.

2 Valley fold the strip end to end and unfold.

3 Valley fold the strip edge to edge and unfold.

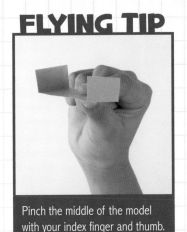

Pinch the middle of the model with your index finger and thumb. Release with a gentle forward push. The higher you hold it, the longer it will flutter.

6 Finished Whirly

END HERE

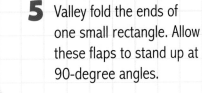

5 Valley fold the ends of one small rectangle. Allow these flaps to stand up at 90-degree angles.

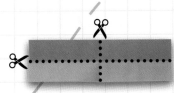

4 Cut the strip on the creases made in steps 2 and 3.

As an airplane moves forward through the sky, a force called **drag** pushes against it. Tiny air molecules rub against the plane and cause drag. Drag always works in the opposite direction of a moving object.

RING WING

Traditional Model

The Ring Wing looks more like a napkin ring than a paper airplane. But this circular glider really sails.

Materials

* 6-inch (15-cm) square of paper

START HERE

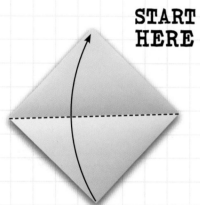

1 Valley fold point to point.

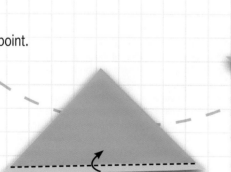

2 Valley fold the edge to create a narrow strip.

3 Valley fold again.

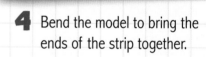

4 Bend the model to bring the ends of the strip together.

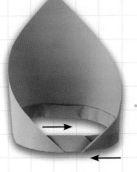

5 Tuck one end of the strip inside the other as far as it will go.

FLYING TIP

Hold the pointed end of the wing with your index finger and thumb. Release the Ring Wing with a gentle, forward push. Hold it high when you launch it to make it glide farther.

If something is **streamlined**, it has smooth edges, with few parts sticking out. Airplanes are streamlined. They have round, smooth noses and wheels that tuck inside the plane when in flight to reduce the amount of drag.

6 Shape the ring into a smooth circle.

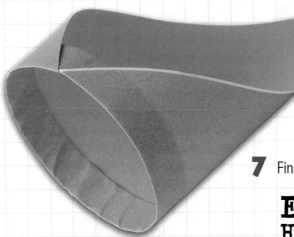

7 Finished Ring Wing

END HERE

FLYING SQUIRREL

Traditional Model

This glider is nothing more than a single wing. But gravity and air currents give it amazing flights. With the right push, the model will glide like a graceful flying squirrel.

Materials

* 6-inch (15-cm) square of paper

START HERE

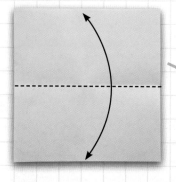

1 Valley fold edge to edge and unfold.

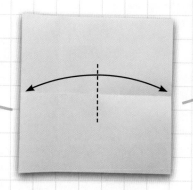

2 Mark fold edge to edge and unfold.

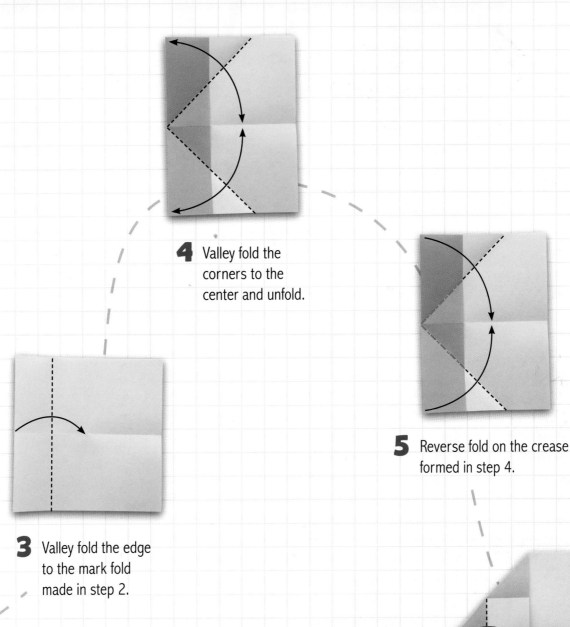

4 Valley fold the corners to the center and unfold.

5 Reverse fold on the crease formed in step 4.

3 Valley fold the edge to the mark fold made in step 2.

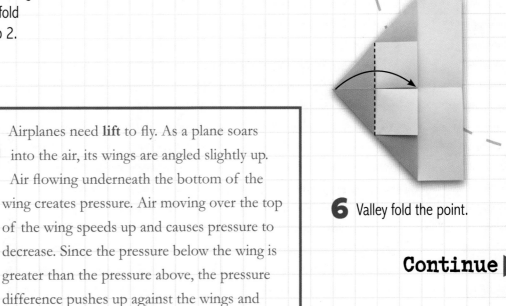

6 Valley fold the point.

Airplanes need **lift** to fly. As a plane soars into the air, its wings are angled slightly up. Air flowing underneath the bottom of the wing creates pressure. Air moving over the top of the wing speeds up and causes pressure to decrease. Since the pressure below the wing is greater than the pressure above, the pressure difference pushes up against the wings and creates lift.

Continue ▶

8 Mountain fold the model in half and unfold.

9 Finished Flying Squirrel

END
HERE

7 Valley fold the flaps and tuck them into the pockets of the point.

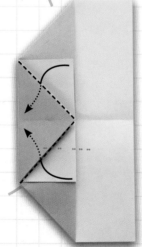

FLYING TIP

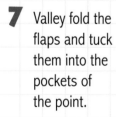

Pinch the back end of the wing with your index finger and thumb. Release with a gentle, forward push. The higher you hold it at launch, the farther it will glide.

HELICOPTER

Traditional Model

With a snip here and a fold there, you'll make the paper Helicopter in less than three minutes. This classic toy never ceases to amaze. Go ahead, give it a whirl!

Materials

* 8.5- by 11-inch (22- by 28-cm) paper
* scissors
* large paper clip

START HERE

1 Cut a 3.5-inch (9-cm) strip off the paper's long side.

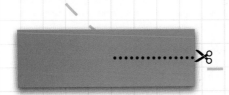

2 Cut a 5-inch (13-cm) slit down the center of the strip.

4 Valley fold the flaps.

Continue ▶

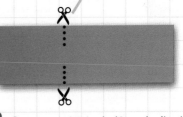

3 Cut two 1.25-inch (3-cm) slits in the sides of the strip. These slits should be about 4 inches (10 cm) from the bottom of the strip.

6 Add a paper clip to the folded edge.

5 Valley fold the bottom edge.

7 Valley fold one propeller. Mountain fold the other propeller.

The main **rotor** on top of a helicopter works like a wing of an airplane. The difference is that the main rotor turns to create airflow, whereas airplane wings rely on the entire plane to move through the air. As air flows over and under the rotor, the pressure created on the bottom of the rotor is higher than the pressure on top. The higher pressure under the rotor pushes up and creates lift.

END HERE

8 Finished Helicopter

TAILSPIN

Traditional Model

Some paper airplanes land smoothly. But the Tailspin prefers crash landings. With a hard throw, this model spins wildly through the air and crashes in a blaze of glory.

Materials

* 8.5- by 11-inch (22- by 28-cm) paper

START HERE

Continue ▶

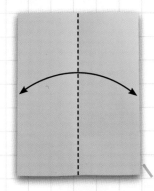

1 Valley fold edge to edge and unfold.

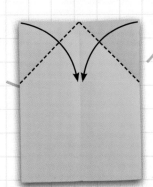

2 Valley fold the corners to the center.

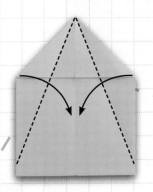

3 Valley fold the edges to the center.

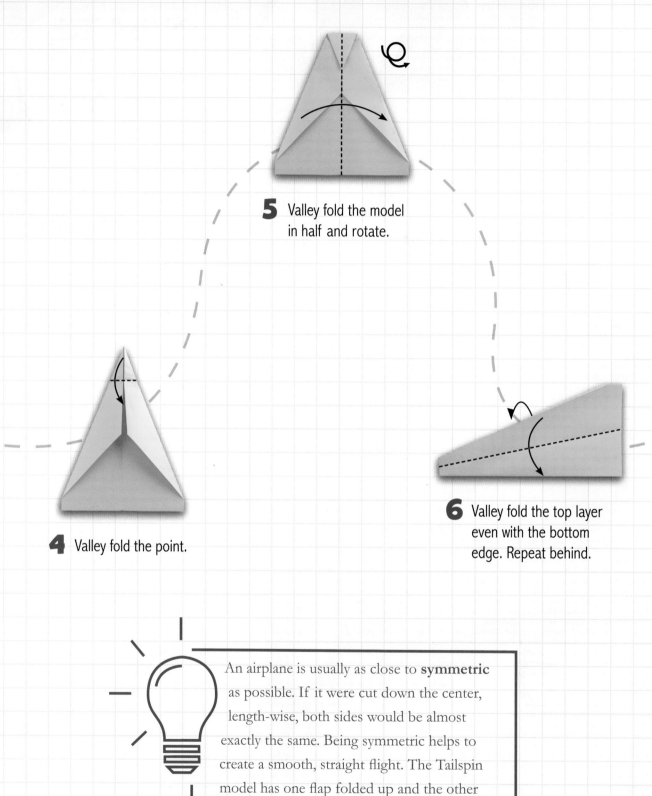

5 Valley fold the model in half and rotate.

4 Valley fold the point.

6 Valley fold the top layer even with the bottom edge. Repeat behind.

An airplane is usually as close to **symmetric** as possible. If it were cut down the center, length-wise, both sides would be almost exactly the same. Being symmetric helps to create a smooth, straight flight. The Tailspin model has one flap folded up and the other folded down. This asymmetric design sends the plane into a spin.

Use a strong throw with a slight upward angle.

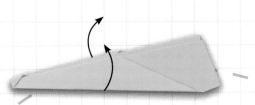

7 Lift the wings.

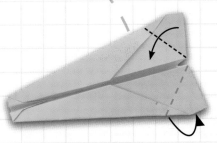

8 Valley fold one corner up slightly. Mountain fold the other corner down slightly.

9 Finished Tailspin

END HERE

LONG RANGER

Traditional Model

The Long Ranger has no equal. It flies farther and straighter than any other model in this book. With the right throw, it can cover distances of 45 feet (14 meters). That's something to remember when your school has a paper airplane contest!

Materials

* 8.5- by 11-inch (22- by 28-cm) paper

START HERE

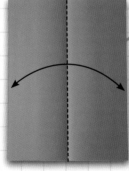

1 Valley fold edge to edge and unfold.

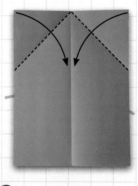

2 Valley fold the corners to the center.

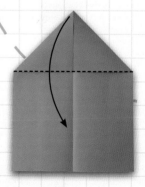

3 Valley fold the point.

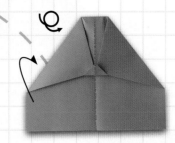

5 Valley fold the point.

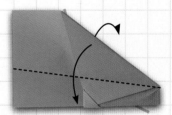

6 Mountain fold the model in half and rotate.

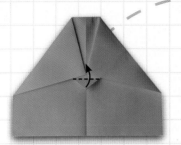

4 Valley fold the corners to the center.

7 Valley fold the top layer even with the bottom edge. Repeat behind.

Continue ▶

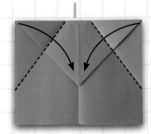

Wind affects how an airplane flies. When a plane flies in the same direction as the wind (a tailwind), it will fly a longer distance. Pilots use tailwinds to help their planes fly farther with less energy. Taking off into the wind (a headwind) can give a plane lift and help it climb better because of the faster air speed flowing over the wings.

END
HERE

9 Finished Long Ranger

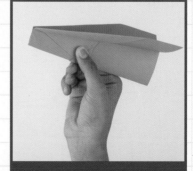

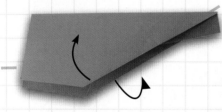

8 Lift the wings.

FLYING TIP

Use a medium throw with a slight upward angle.

ELEVATOR GLIDER

Traditional Model

If you like to tinker with flight patterns, the Elevator Glider is just for you. Adjust the angles of the flaps to find the flight that fits you right.

Materials

* 8.5- by 11-inch (22- by 28-cm) paper
* scissors

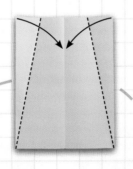

START HERE

1 Valley fold edge to edge and unfold.

2 Valley fold the corners to the center. Note how the creases end at the bottom corners of the paper.

Continue ▶

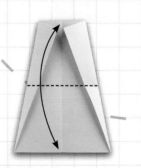

3 Valley fold in half and unfold.

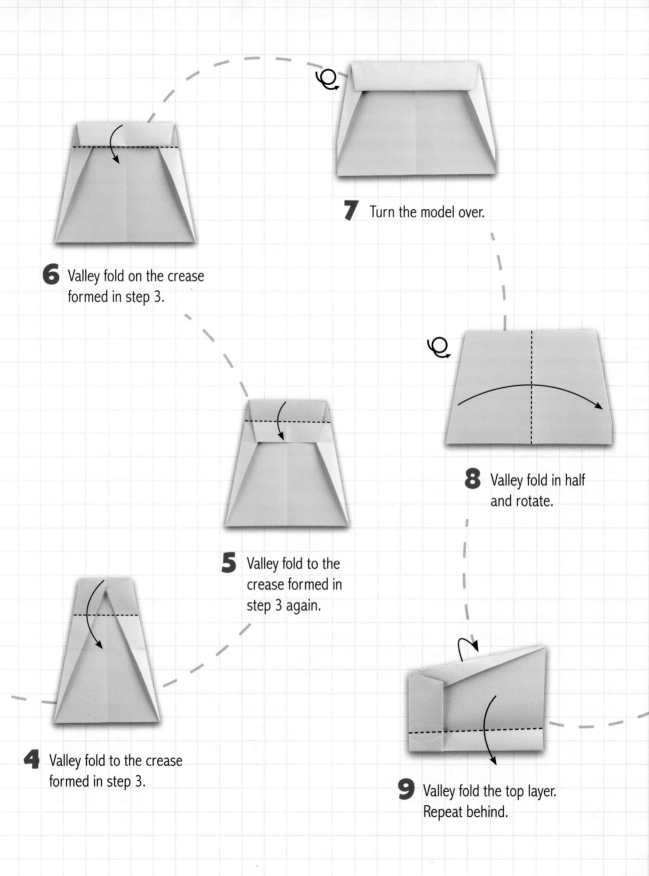

6 Valley fold on the crease formed in step 3.

7 Turn the model over.

8 Valley fold in half and rotate.

5 Valley fold to the crease formed in step 3 again.

4 Valley fold to the crease formed in step 3.

9 Valley fold the top layer. Repeat behind.

Flaps change the flow of air around an airplane and the direction of air forces pushing on it. A plane with flaps folded up on the back creates a force pushing down on the tail, which lifts the front. That's why the movable surface on the tail is called an elevator — it can cause up or down movement, just like an elevator!

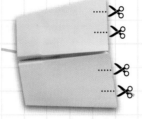

10 Lift the wings.

11 Cut a flap in the back of each wing. Angle the flaps upward slightly.

12 Finished Elevator Glider

END HERE

INSIDE THE HANGAR:
The Wright Brothers' 1902 Glider

Two American brothers, Wilbur and Orville Wright, invented the first fully controllable aircraft in the world — the 1902 glider. But their journey to create this incredible flying craft was filled with unexpected problems and lots of crash landings! One of the biggest challenges the Wright brothers faced was finding a reliable way to control the craft's steering. After many test flights, they decided to try a rear rudder.

(A plane rudder acts much like the rudder on a ship — it controls the direction of the craft.) Fortunately, their clever rudder idea worked. Finally the pilot could control his craft in three directions: roll (up and down movement of the wing tips), pitch (up and down movement of the plane's nose), and yaw (side to side movement of the plane's nose).

The 1902 glider was the first of the Wright brothers' gliders to include a rudder.

The Wright brothers' glider had two 32-feet (9.8-m) wings. It didn't have any seats. Instead, the pilot lay down on the bottom wing and held on tight to the controls. Built out of wood and strong fabric, the Wright brothers' glider weighed only 117 pounds (53 kilograms).

READ MORE

Collins, John M. *The New World Champion Paper Airplane Book: Featuring the Guinness World Record-Breaking Design, with Tear-Out Planes to Fold and Fly.* New York: Ten Speed Press, 2013.

LaFosse, Michael G. *Michael LaFosse's Origami Airplanes.* North Clarendon, Vt.: Tuttle Publishing, 2016.

Lee, Kyong Hwa. *Amazing Paper Airplanes: The Craft and Science of Flight.* Albuquerque, N.Mex.: University of New Mexico Press, 2016.

INTERNET SITES

Use FactHound to find Internet sites related to this book.

Visit *www.facthound.com*

Just type in 9781543507973 and go.

Special thanks to our adviser, Polly Kadolph, Associate Professor,
University of Dubuque (Iowa) Aviation Department, for her expertise.

Dabble Lab Books are published by Capstone Press,
1710 Roe Crest Drive, North Mankato, Minnesota 56003
www.mycapstone.com

Library of Congress Cataloging-in-Publication data is available on the Library of Congress website.
ISBN: 978-1-5435-0797-3 (library binding)
ISBN: 978-1-5435-0801-7 (eBook PDF)

Summary: Send your readers flying down the runway with a simple fold, fold, fold, and a side of science.
Step-by-step instructions show budding flight-school students how to build the Spinning Blimp and other
beginning-level paper airplanes, while hearty, fact-filled sidebars and an "Inside the Hangar" feature explain
basic flight concepts. Engaging 4D components really give this title wings!

Editorial Credits
Jill Kalz, editor; Heidi Thompson, designer; Eric Gohl, media researcher; Laura Manthe, production specialist

Photo Credits
Capstone Studio: Karon Dubke, all steps
Library of Congress: 30
Shutterstock: design elements

Printed in the United States of America.
010761S18